© **Copyright 2017 -MAV4LIF reserved.**

The contents of this book may not b or transmitted without direct writ author.

Under no circumstances will any legal responsibility or blame be held against the publisher for any reparation, damages, or monetary loss due to the information herein, either directly or indirectly.

Legal Notice:

This book is copyright protected. This is only for personal use. You cannot amend, distribute, sell, use, quote or paraphrase any part or the content within this book without the consent of the author.

Disclaimer Notice:

Please note the information contained within this document is for educational and entertainment purposes only. Every attempt has been made to provide accurate, up to date and reliable complete information. No warranties of any kind are expressed or implied. Readers acknowledge that the author is not engaging in the rendering of legal, financial, medical or professional advice. The content of this book has been derived from various sources. Please consult a licensed professional before attempting any techniques outlined in this book.

By reading this document, the reader agrees that under no circumstances are is the author responsible for any losses, direct or indirect, which are incurred as a result of the use of information contained within this document, including, but not limited to, —errors, omissions, or inaccuracies

Dog Workout!

A Complete Schedule of Exercise for Your Dog

By: MAV4LIFE®

ABOUT MAV4LIFE®

"Mav4Life®, is the ultimate resource for dog owners. From free dog training e-books, to toys that will provide your furry friend with hours of enjoyment, we are all about the animals. Learn more on our website: www.mav4life.com, blog and keep up with the fun daily by liking us on Facebook & Instagram @Mav4LifeDogToys

Tail Wags & Sloppy Kisses, Team Mav4Life®"

Make sure you grab your Mav4Life® product today! And give your best friend the quality they deserve! For your FREE GIFT Check out our website!

Table of Contents

Introduction 9
Chapter 1 Walks 13
Chapter 2 The Swimmer 17
Chapter 3 Social Play 21
Chapter 4 Fetch the Ball or the Stick 27
Chapter 5 Creating a simple Agility Course 31
Chapter 6 Knowing your dog's strengths and weaknesses 41
Chapter 7 Equipment you may want to invest in 45
Conclusion 51

Introduction

When you introduce a dog into your home, you take on a responsibility. That dog needs to be treated in the right way and his health needs should be catered for at all times. That means that you should have a good understanding of training, that you know the right foods to give him and that you are able to enjoy a well-behaved animal. Much of the training that you give your dog is necessary. However, what about his exercise once he has been trained? Just like children, dogs need exercise to try and stave off many of the medical conditions that can arise out of lack of activity.

You must have seen movies where lap dogs sit on their mistress's knee and are fed chocolates. Of course, a responsible dog owner will already be aware that feeding dogs with the right kind of nourishment is essential. These are not animals who should be encouraged to eat human foods, unless also suitable for dogs. However, what about the exercise that your dog needs? Have you attended to that? This book gives you a guide of the kind of exercises that you can incorporate into your dog's life, but it does more than that. Certain breeds of dog need different types of exercise and in fact, if you try to introduce the wrong kind of exercise to the wrong breed, you can actually be contributing to the ill health of that dog. Thus, it pays to know what you are doing.

This book has been written by an expert in dog health and the exercises that are contained in this keep fit manual for dogs also takes account of the age of your dog and the breed. From day one, you will be able to incorporate exercise and have fun doing it, because this involves some participation from you. There are many obedience classes for dogs, where dogs are taught to find their way through sets of hurdles, but did you know you can set these up in your own yard? With the right kind of temptation, your dog will be more than happy to join in the fun. This guide shows you how to encourage your dog to exercise in the healthiest of ways and to gain as much pleasure from the experience as you do!

Remember that young puppies have a lot more energy and if you find that your dog does not respond to one of the exercises shown, there are others than they may enjoy. Never force the dog to do anything that makes the dog uncomfortable. You wouldn't do that to your child and ownership responsibility is much the same as parental responsibility. Follow me through the pages of exercises and enjoy having fun with your healthy dog.

Chapter 1
Walks

If you want your dog to stay healthy, the first consideration has to be that the dog will need to "go outside" on a regular basis. It isn't enough to allow the dog into the back yard. Walking with the dog is very important from several perspectives. One if helps you to be able to control the dog on the leash and the other is that this daily exercise helps him to work off all of the calories that he gains from the food that he eats. Dogs who are not encouraged to walk on a regular basis can become overweight and unhealthy, as walking is a natural part of the dog's life. Therefore, it's important to take the dog for its daily walk and a very energetic and larger dog will need to be walked several times a day.

There are several approaches to the walk. If you live in an

area that is urban, you won't have as much freedom as you may in the country, but the dog does need to be able to walk and run a little without the leash. Thus, choose somewhere safe. Your dog needs to be socialized with other dogs and if this has not yet been done, don't let him off his leash. The best way forward is to socialize the dog and get him accustomed to other dogs and this can be done during visits to relatives or during disciplined training while walking in the park. Being with other dogs should not cause him to become fierce and if you have any trouble at all with this area of his training, it's a good idea to go to classes so that he becomes more accustomed to being with other dogs.

<u>Off the leash</u>

If you let a dog off his leash, chances are that he is going to run off, but if you have trained him to come to your call and to obey you, then there is no problem at all with this. The dog may enjoy running ahead of you, but you need to keep your eye on him. There are several things to beware of. For instance, in the country, is the dog liable to trouble sheep or cattle? If so, then you can't let him off the leash. Choose an area which is used for recreation rather than being somewhere where the dog can cause bother to other animals.

Let him go and then call him back and when he comes back, treat him. That will keep him pretty near you because dogs know where those treats are. Be aware of your dog's limits as smaller dogs may overdo it and can be let off the leash in the back yard for exercise rather than in places where there may be animals larger than the dog.

Running together

This can be a great exercise for a mature dog whose behavior is good in public places. You will find that your dog will take your lead if he is a natural runner and can easily keep up with you. When you stop to rest, pat the dog and make a fuss of him. It's always a good idea to keep your dog aware that he has been a good dog because this keeps up his impetus to please you. Carry along a few treats.

If you are new to running with your dog, keep your treats in the pocket away from where he is standing but make him aware that they are there. Feed him a treat and then start to run and he will naturally follow you, thinking that there are more treats to come. You need to get the balance right so that the dog wants to follow you rather than always expecting treats, but the treats are there to help to train him into wanting to be your running companion.

The types of routes you choose when you run together

dictate the danger level. For example, keep away from roads. It may be common sense to you to keep away from roads, but it's not such a commonsense idea to the dog and accidents can happen.

If you are worried about the safety of your dog, go to large parks which have plenty of running space and stay inside the boundaries of the park. Remember that hot weather affects your dog as much as it affects you. Your dog will need to stop for water if you intend to go on long runs, so be aware of these needs and don't overwork the dog. It's supposed to be fun.

Chapter 2
The Swimmer

Not all dogs are natural swimmers. The type of dogs that are include Golden Retrievers, springer spaniels, Labradors and poodles. If you intend to go swimming with your dog or to throw a stick toward the river so that the dog can retrieve it, you need to be aware that dogs are not very sensible when it comes to creating their own boundaries. Many of these breeds love swimming, but they don't know when it's wise to stop.

If you are not a swimmer yourself, then keep this kind of activity to areas where the water currents are not too strong. That way, your dog will not be pulled away by the current. You need to choose somewhere where entry into the water and exit from the water is relatively easy. In nature parks, you will often find small beach areas and these are ideal because they give the dog an easy entry and exit point from the water. Even a ramp in boating ponds is easy enough for the dog to use or indeed steps.

Dogs who are swimmers will enjoy the cardio vascular benefits of swimming just like humans do. It exercises their body in a very non-impact way and is an extremely healthy exercise. However, if you have never done this before with the dog, approach with caution. Find a safe place to try. Walk down to the edge of the water and sit for a while and see how the dog reacts to the water. Perhaps he will walk to the edge in curiosity. Perhaps he will even paddle to a certain extent. When you throw a stick for him to retrieve, throw it toward the edge of the water so that you can gage how he responds to this.

Then try throwing the stick a little further. You will know immediately whether your dog is a swimmer or not because some dogs, other than the breeds mentioned, really do not like the water at all, so never force a dog to do something against his nature.

Things to watch out for

Limit the amount of time that the dog spends in the water to about ten minutes at first and then call the dog toward you. Keep the dog within sight at all times. If you notice that the dog is struggling, you do need to be there to help him to make his way to the shore.

Chapter 3
Social Play

If you put a load of kids together in the back yard, chances are that they will soon be playing together. Socialization is very important for dogs from several viewpoints. The first is that while you are out walking, you will come across other dogs and your dog needs to know how to behave when this happens. A socialized dog will have a better idea of what is expected of him and will not attack other dogs. Thus, socialization is encouraged. It's also encouraged from another viewpoint. Dogs love to play together. If you have friends who have dogs, it's a good idea to get together to get the dogs accustomed to each other's company.

You will find that dogs who are unafraid will play together

and this kind of social activity is extremely important for the dog. It is spontaneous play and chasing and can even involve a certain amount of fun wrestling, but before you can get to this stage, the dog needs to be taught to accept other dogs. The sooner you get your dog socialized the better and you can start this kind of training at the age of four to twelve weeks old. This is the ideal learning window, but many people miss this period because they get their dog from a rescue service when the dog is older or did not get a chance to train them at this age. That doesn't mean it's too late to start. It just means it will take a little more concentrated effort on your part to train the dog to accept others.

Taking your dog out with a friend who has another dog is a great opportunity. Remember when you are out walking, the walk itself will wear down the energy of the dog making the dog a little more submissive than usual and that works in your favor. In the early days of socialization, you need to keep the dog on the leash so that you can correct behavior that is unsuitable. A gentle tug on the leash can stop your dog from being anti-social. However, shouting at the dog is not the answer since this can excite him even more. Be firm but be reasonably quiet in your discipline. Simply pulling the leash in a jerk movement to pull him away from a dog should be enough. You can also use treats after the fact to show the dog that he has done the right thing.

Socializing a dog correctly

Some owners are under the impression that you can socialize a dog simply by placing the dog with other dogs. This is a huge mistake because you may be instilling fear into the dog when the socialization process should be a positive experience that introduces the dog to things that he finds pleasant. The best way to do this when you first take your dog out to walk is to skirt around the park, so that the dog can see other dogs in the distance, but has the security blanket of the fence around the park. Little by little the dog gets accustomed to being in the company of other dogs, rather than being thrown in at the deep end.

Escape from a potential threat

The mistake that many people make when trying to socialize dogs is placing them in a situation where there is little escape from potential fights. The dog may fear confrontation but fear isn't necessarily a good thing from a discipline point of view because a scared dog reacts in an undisciplined way. You need to make sure that the first socialization is done in a place where the dog feels safe. Although some people like to send their dogs to classes where the dog is forced to socialize with other dogs, it's a far better practice to have private coaching lessons first. This deals with the interaction between the dog and the owner and this is vital when you are considering socialization. If you don't have that right in the first place, the dog can be in danger when in the company of other dogs. A few private sessions can fix this because you learn to understand your dog better and your dog learns the importance of understanding you. This means that when faced with other dogs, he will first of all react to your instructions rather than going into panic mode. It's important that you have built this trust between you so that the dog is not afraid and has the confidence that you can help him to escape danger.

Socialization bit by bit

If you have family members with a dog or cat, go to visit regularly and get your dog accustomed to the presence of other animals in a controlled environment. Little by little, increase the social aspect but be aware that your first priority should be the dog. You can't afford to take your eyes off him if he is not accustomed to dealing with other animals. Gradually increase this exposure to other dogs and as he gained his comfort levels, you will find that your dog and the dogs he knows will want to play together and that this will give him a whole load of exercise. If you hear growling that is not aggressive, chances are that your dog is enjoying a good wrestle with a friend, rather than being in any danger. However, be aware of your dog's activities at all times and be ready with the whistle or a clicker if you feel that the behavior needs to stop. If you have a large dog, often play can be misinterpreted as aggression by children, so make sure that children are aware that the dog is playing rather than being aggressive. Children need to recognize the dog's behavior so that they do not try to stop the fun.

Chapter 4
Fetch the Ball or the Stick

This is a trick that many dogs are familiar with but you may not know that the energy used by the dog is giving the dog healthy exercise. If you do have a dog who is a natural at going to get that stick, you are fortunate because you don't need to put the dog through too much training. If your dog is the type to sit and ignore the throwing of the stick, then you may need to spend more time trying to train the dog. You may find that the dog responds better to a ball or to a chew toy. After all, there is more incentive for the dog to bring back the chew toy than there is to bring back a stick.

Familiarizing the dog with a toy
Some dogs don't catch on as quickly as other dogs, but you

can help the process along a bit by introducing the dog to the toy. The moment the dog bends to sniff the toy or acknowledge that the toy is there, you can either use a click trainer to acknowledge that you noticed or a simple treat and a pat on the head. Remember that in the initial stages, this is merely introducing your pet to something new. You don't have to treat a dog when he has learned a new exercise and does it as a matter of course.

Hold the toy in your hand. The idea is to get the dog interested in it. Hold it toward his face and only reward and click when the dog's nose actually sniffs the toy and shows an interest in it. The next step is fun. Place the toy on the ground next to the dog and place your hand cupped upward ready to receive the toy. Most dogs will know by instinct what it is that you want and will pick up the toy and place it in your hand. Encourage the dog and if this happens, treat him.

<u>Introducing an element of fun</u>

Dogs don't always see the fun that you do in the toys that you get for them. The best way to introduce a new toy is to place his existing toys in a circle. Get him interested in one of them and then take another one and play with it on your own. His curiosity will eventually make him wonder what fun he is missing. Make your interaction with the toy sound really good fun and use excited tones and your dog will soon be curious enough to want the toy you are playing with. Then take the next one and do the same thing. What's happening is that your dog is getting accustomed to the scent of the toys but is also associating each of the toys with fun behavior.

From this introduction, you can simply take all of the toys away and then choose one to throw, enthusing the puppy to go and fetch the toy. Since he is accustomed to playing with you, it will be natural for him to bring the toy back to you.

<u>Getting the dog to let go of the toy and give it to you</u>
If you stand still and merely give a command, some dogs will respond with obedience, but since the toy is his, it's much more likely that the dog will hold the toy in his mouth and will not want to let go of it. Show him a treat but don't give it to him and follow this with the word "Give!" holding out your other hand to take the toy. If he doesn't get it, show him the treat again. You can bet that the treat is more interesting than the toy.

Repeat the action. Show the treat and then put it away and immediately ask the dog to "Give" holding your hand out to take the toy from him. If he responds in the correct way and gives you the toy, you give him the treat. Dogs are very fast to catch on especially when they know that there is a treat in store for them. Never give the treat before the toy is dropped into your hand because this sends mixed messages and the dog will not know what he is supposed to be doing. Your behavior when you deal with dogs has to be completely consistent.

You can usually graduate from this type of play to using sticks. The dog will already be accustomed to running and retrieving his toys and it's a natural extension to this that he will recognize that you want him to fetch when you throw a stick. This is a great exercise for your dog when you are in a countryside situation. Perhaps you have stopped for a barbecue in someone's large garden. Perhaps you are simply out in the country. Be aware of dangers if there are a lot of people around. The best area for this type of activity really is the open countryside where there are plenty of sticks and also plenty of room for the dog to chase sticks without upsetting anyone in the vicinity.

If you do it right, you can guarantee that this will be an exercise your dog will expect every time you go for a walk in the woods!

Chapter 5
Creating a simple Agility Course

One of the reasons that people use a clicker for training is that the dog recognizes the click even if there are other sounds in the area, and it means that he will get a treat because he has done something right. These can be used for getting your dog to use an agility course in your back yard. However, there is something you need to be aware of. Never use the clicker just for the sake of it. It is vital that this is only used as a reward gesture or the dog will become confused. The clicker denotes the good act and then the dog is rewarded. This is a good method for training your dog and is helpful in the case of agility training. This is not only good exercise for him, but it is also good fun for you and your pet as a bonding exercise. Once your pet has learned how to navigate the agility course, you won't need to treat him all the time. A simply pat on the head or letting the dog know you are pleased will be enough. However, in the training stages it's essential.

You can use a simple object like a log or something that the dog needs to jump over to start your course and to teach him to jump. Take the dog on the leash because this gives you better control and lead him around the yard until he is faced by the log. Use the word "Up!" or some other simple word that denotes jump! The simpler you keep your words the better because dogs won't understand sentences. Shout "Up!" and pull on the leash a little bit so he gets the point and jumps over the log. Click and reward.

Now add two logs or two hurdles and continue to walk in a circle doing the same thing every time that you get to a log. In my brother's case, he found that jumping the log with the dog helped, but this largely depends upon the character of your dog. Some dogs don't need that example while others will find it useful.

As your dog gets more and more accustomed to the logs, add more and go around the course, clicking and treating every time he jumps over the logs. Now try it off the leash by simply calling the dog and starting to run around the course. If you dog is a playful dog, chances are that he will follow you and do the same things that you do. Click and treat.

Adding a tunnel

A child's play tunnel can be used to train the dog to go through tunnels, but it must be sufficiently large so that the dog can get through it fairly comfortably. You can create one from all kinds of things, but be sure that the fabric it is made of has no sharp edges that can harm the dog. You also need to be aware that dogs do not naturally go into a tunnel because they fear what is hiding down the tunnel and are wiser than that. Thus, when you set up the tunnel, make sure that light can be seen at the other end so going through it is a fun exercise rather than a step into the dark. You can make the tunnel part of your running circle around the back yard, alternating with logs so that your dog gets the point that it's all part and parcel of the fun.

Training with the tunnel

In the same way as with other training, you need to encourage your dog to go through the tunnel. I found one of the best ways is to place the dog at the entry to the tunnel and say "Stay!" Then, go to the other end of the tunnel so that the dog can see you through the tunnel and say "Come!" The quickest way to come to you will be through the tunnel and the fact that you are there will help to alleviate any fears that the dog may have. You may find that the dog takes a little while to get it and will come around the side of the tunnel. In this case, merely place him back at the beginning and start again. If the dog finds a tunnel too long or daunting, try with a cardboard box with both ends open so that he can run through it. The major thing to remember is that you must click and treat when he achieves what it is that you want him to do. That is the instantly recognizable sign to him that he did something right.

Now try the agility course again, this time with logs to jump over and tunnels to go through. Make it fun rather than hard work and never try to get your dog to do this when the dog is too tired. It won't work because the dog needs enthusiasm in order to achieve this kind of activity. The types of dog who are particularly good with this kind of activity are those who have shorter legs, such as Pugs, terriers, bulldogs and even dogs as small as Shi Tzus. I have trained a Chihuahua to do this as well but it will take patience. The other thing you need to remember with any dog is that dogs can overheat. Thus never push your dog so far that this happens. Make sure that there is water available for the dog at all times during hot weather.

Steps and slides

Some puppies will respond well to climbing up steps and sliding down slides but not all will. It will take a little patience but if you place your hand above the steps the dog will usually get the message that you want him to rise up and will learn that the steps will help him to do that. For the slide, you simply wait at the bottom or can even encourage the dog from the side of the slide by tapping on the slide bed so that he knows you want him to go there. The dog may find the sensation of sliding a little strange at first, but when you click and treat him, chances are that he will get over his initial fears when he sees that no harm comes to him by doing this activity.

A child using the slide can also be a great motivator as the dog will copy.

The slalom

This is very easy to set up. Get the kids to paint plastic mineral water bottles and half fill them with sand. Place these in a row. The best way to get the dog to use the slalom correctly is with the lead because you can more or less direct the dog over the top of the slalom so he knows which way to go as he zigzags around the bottles.

- Click and treat.

- Do it again.

- Click and treat.

It will take a while before you will be able to get the dog to do this without the lead but persevere for as long as the dog remains interested. If the dog gets bored with the idea, it's no longer fun and it makes for difficult training. Thus, stop and never force the dog to do anything that's too hard when he is tired.

There are all sorts of obstacles that you can use for your agility course. I have used a see-saw which was made from a plank and an oil drum. I have also created all kinds of obstacles from pieces of wood or children's toys and you can evolve this gradually as you introduce your dog to each of the exercises that involve that particular piece of equipment. Remember to use things that are safe and to pack it all away when you have finished. Then, the next time you are out in the back yard with the dog and he sees all the equipment coming out, he will be impatient to enjoy showing off his skills. Be patient and loving with your dog and never force him to work beyond his own comfort levels. If you make a dog do that, it is likely that you will not get a positive response during training. The dog needs to see the activities that are introduced as being positive activities rather than punishment. At the end of the session, make sure that your dog is given a drink and that he is patted to show him that you are pleased with his progress.

When getting your dog to use the agility course, never confuse the signals. For example, if you choose to use a whistle, stick with the whistle. If you choose to use a clicker, click it only when you want to reward the dog for something he has done. Confusion of these signals will not help you to train the dog so don't click or whistle unless you are absolutely sure that it's the right time.

<u>Use of a whistle</u>

In the equipment section of this book, we have advised people that they can use a whistle as this is a great tool to communicate with your dog. The tones of the whistle and the numbers of whistles can denote different things. If you were to watch a sheepdog at work, you would know straight away that the obedience level of these dogs is amazing. However, you do need to get the whistle at the right pitch for your dog to be able to hear it. This is why we recommend an adjustable whistle and have it adjusted before you start your session. You will find that a good quality whistle will have instructions with it on how to adjust the sound and will show you how you need to do that to suit your dog.

The agility course that you set up for your dog should incorporate different activities but you need to train the dog in each activity singularly. If you try to get your dog to understand too much at the same time, it can confuse the dog. Thus, teach each of the activities on their own and once they have been achieved and done several times, move onto the next activity. You will find that you will be able to design new activities to include in your agility course, based upon your progress and the dog's response to the training so far. If a dog responds well to obstacles for example, you can make the difficulty level more intensive as the dog gains in experience. Instead of using one log, for example, use two or even make the height or width of the obstacle larger so that the dog needs to use more vigorous exercise to get over that obstacle. It is hard to give exact instructions in this, because it really depends upon the reaction of your dog to the obstacles you are introducing. On a hot summer's day, you can also introduce a water obstacle which will be fun for water loving dogs. You will soon find out if your dog hates water! Whatever you use as a hurdle in your agility course, be aware of the potential of hurting your dog. It is your responsibility to ensure that the dog is kept safe from injury at all times.

Chapter 6
Knowing your dog's strengths and weaknesses

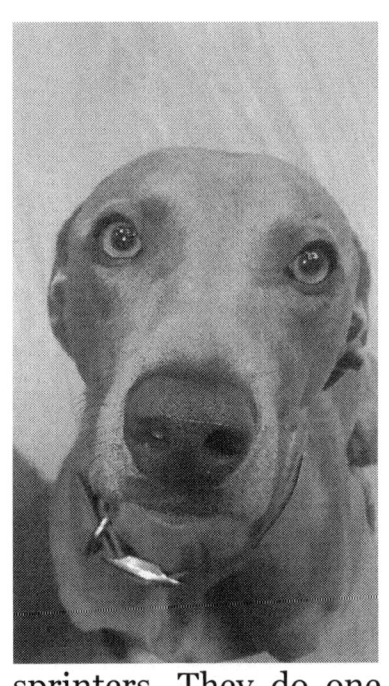

People make the mistake of grouping dogs into different categories and having certain expectations of that particular breed. The example I could give would be greyhounds. These are associated as racing dogs and thus one would assume that running practice is good for them. However, you need to understand that the fact is that these are sprinters. They do one relatively short sprint in a quick amount of time. They are not the kind of dog you should expect to be able to run a marathon. Just because you have a large dog, don't assume that his activity level is going to be higher than that of a small dog. Some dogs that are large only enjoy a moderate amount of exercise. The other thing to bear in mind is that the thickness of his coat may have a bearing upon his activity. For example, chows have a thick coat and can only exercise for about 30 minutes at a time without suffering from heat exhaustion.

Great Danes are also huge dogs that people expect to have stamina. In a case such as this you need to remember that each breed of dog has weak spots. Thus, before exercising or introducing exercise into the life of the dog, it's a good idea to visit the vet and talk about what kind of exercise is best for that particular dog. I say this because Great Danes have a tendency to suffer from hip complaints and knowing what your particular breed of dog is prone to suffer from will help you to design exercises that are suitable for that particular breed.

Bassett hounds and dachshunds should not be subjected to agility training. These are dogs whose backs are long and who have short legs. The difficulty with this kind of dog is that they are prone to disc problems and agility exercises are likely to bring this kind of problem on. Thus, in the case of these dogs, walking and playing is perhaps a better choice of exercise.

Short haired dogs with long legs are usually among the most active of dogs. Pointers and ridgebacks will be capable of most sports and will need a lot of exercise, since their energy levels are high. In the case of a dog of this nature, you do need to have a strict exercise routine because they need that exercise to stay in tip top condition.

<u>Chihuahuas and small dogs</u>

There is a tendency to give this type of dog more treats than other dogs. The toy varieties, however, are not actual toys. Try to limit the amount of scraps you give to small dogs as these will put on unnecessary weight which is bad for their heart and their health in general. Particularly avoid human snacks. If you are going to exercise dogs that are miniatures, you will find that they love running and walking. They also have fun with agility training but don't expect total cooperation.

One of the exercises that modern society has been imposing upon these small breeds is trying to get them to walk on their hind feet only. Sure, it's amusing to see, but not something that should be encouraged too much. It is preferable that you teach dogs like this to say "please" by sitting on their behinds and placing their front paws out, rather than trying to put all of the strain on the hind legs. This can be equally as amusing for your friends and family without endangering the dog.

Chihuahuas were Mexican hunting dogs and were expected to burrow to find their prey. You will find that these dogs are natural diggers, especially in parts of the garden where you don't want them to dig! Thus, training them in agility training should include tunnels as they will find this a very natural and enjoyable exercise. Cardboard tunnels can be extended so that this ups the difficulty level.

You will find that dachshunds who are not given enough exercise can suffer from being overweight and this puts a huge strain on the disks in their back. Thus, if you do take on a pet of this nature, regular walks will become a part of their healthy routine.

In all cases of pet ownership, it's a good idea to take your pet to the vet and to have a regular checkup of the pet so that you can establish what kind of level of activity you can expect from that pet. The vet will also be able to give you information on the types of exercise your dog will be able to indulge in and warn you of the activities to avoid. Listen very carefully to this advice because it's important to the health of your dog.

Chapter 7

Equipment you may want to invest in

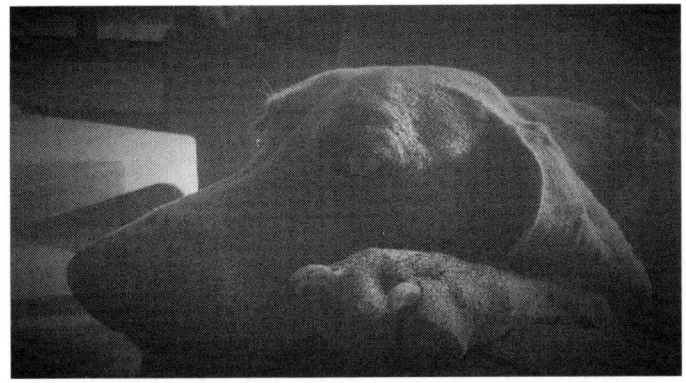

Dog owners will need to have standard equipment for the day to day care of their dogs but there are certain items that are useful when you are exercising your dog. A clicker trainer is a good idea. The dog starts to recognize this as being a congratulatory sound that acknowledges that the dog has done something right as the use of the clicker is associated with treats. They don't cost a lot and come in the form of a keyring fob which is easy to slip into your pocket.

Training and exercise treats

When buying treats, bear in mind the breed of your dog and his preferences. You will usually get to know what your dog really enjoys as treats and these need to be in packets small enough to carry in your pocket to reinforce good behavior. Your pet store will be able to show you what is available and you can try out various treats until you find the right one to enthuse your dog into action!

Dog Toys

There are several items available in your pet store, but the ones that are chewy are particularly good for dogs. These can be used when you throw the toy and expect the dog to retrieve it. It's worth having a collection of toys for training purposes and you may have to renew these after a while but invest in good ones rather than cheap plastic toys that will break or crack and become a danger to kids and to pets alike. Balls are good fun for dogs and these are also washable meaning that you can keep them clean so your kids don't pick up infections.

Leash

It is a good idea to have an extendible leash so that as the dog gets more disciplined, you are able to let him have a little more freedom. These longer leashes are good for when you go jogging together because they are not restricting the dog. A retractable leash is useful in environments where you sense there may be danger and you can slacken off the leash when you know that the danger has passed. They are particularly good for smaller dogs because they may be exposed to danger in a park situation where there are other larger dogs. Using a short leash in these circumstances, you are able to pick up the dog at short notice to keep him safe from potential predators.

Whistle

Some people prefer to use a whistle for while exercising their dogs. This can be helpful during dog socialization especially if you want your dog to calm down. If you are going to use a whistle, you need one with an adjustable pitch because not all dogs can hear the pitch of a standard whistle. If you use one for training your dog, be consistent with what the whistle means by reinforcing positive action with treats.

There are other things that you can buy for your dog, but try to buy those things that are made from dog friendly materials. Quite often a dog will be happy to chew on a dog rope toy rather than a plastic one. Look to see what your pet store has in stock and try to couple the size of the toy with the size of your dog. You will find that your dog will develop a liking for certain items and these can be used during his exercise routines to burn off excess energy!

There are so many different gadgets that you may be tempted to buy to make your activity with your dog pleasurable for him and for yourself. However, do not be fooled into buying cheap gimmick style accessories that you don't need. The dog is more interested in the relationship that he has with his owner and it takes very little equipment to get your dog exercising on a regular basis. More toys and gadgets are likely to cause more confusion. When you are setting up an agility course for your dog, of course you can buy agility course items but these can be made at home and you don't have to spend a fortune. Cardboard boxes make great obstacles and tunnels. If your kids are learning to play with your dog, then encourage the kids to come up with safe ideas that can be used during the exercise sessions.

You also need to teach your kids the idea behind using the clicker so that they are not tempted to click it for the sake of it. The dog will become confused if this is done. This should only be used as a sign that the dog has done something right and should be followed by a small treat. One of the biggest mistakes that people make when trying to introduce their dogs to an exercise schedule is lack of consistency. If you want your dog to respond to your commands and do what it is that you want him to do, consistency is vital to the equation.

Conclusion

Any of the exercises within this program can be adapted to suit your pet. For example, you will know if your dog is a good climber or not and can eliminate climbing from the agility course if you feel that this is too much for your dog. Since the dog is considered to be a member of the family, during your initial training period, you will have noticed the kind of things that the dog likes. You can use all of this information to help you to make his exercise routine enjoyable and fun for the dog, rather than being seen as being some kind of punishment. If your dog is too tired to exercise, then this isn't a good time to introduce new ideas.

Remember that extreme weather conditions may also present difficulty for your pet. You need to make sure that your dog is hydrated and that he has plenty of water available for him to drink in hot weather. This is absolutely essential. You also need to be sure that your dog is the kind of breed to be encouraged to swim, since certain breeds do not respond well to this kind of activity. Your vet will know the answers to all of your questions about the breed of dog that you are exercising.

Since exercise is used to keep your dog fit, you are discouraged from using treats that are unhealthy. Buy special dog treats that are good for the teeth and bones and that your dog enjoys, rather than using human treats.

As well as exercise, your dog needs all of the nourishment of good quality food and will also need rest. Thus, remember that just as all of these elements are important to humans, a balance of them is important for your dog. Try to encourage your dog by making exercise something that is enjoyed. Walking twice a day with the dog can help him to get accustomed to the leash and obedience training will help when you find yourself in a situation where other dogs are present. It is advised that you go back over the book and start to introduce daily walking, agility exercises, swimming, retrieving and all of the suggestions in this book to your pet. As you introduce a new element into his daytime routine, remember that your praise and your participation are important to him. With this element in place, you can look forward to years of pleasure with your dog. And remember, above all else, that if you are ill and cannot exercise your dog, it may be worthwhile enlisting the help of a neighbor or someone who loves dogs as much as you do to ensure that the dog's exercise routine is not neglected.

"Mav4Life®, is the ultimate resource for dog owners. From free dog training e-books, to toys that will provide your furry friend with hours of enjoyment, we are all about the animals. Learn more on our website: www.mav4life.com, blog and keep up with the fun daily by liking us on Facebook & Instagram @Mav4LifeDogToys

Tail Wags & Sloppy Kisses, Team Mav4Life®"

Make sure you grab your Mav4Life® product today! And give your best friend the quality they deserve! For your FREE GIFT Check out our website!

Printed in Great Britain
by Amazon